Written and Illustrated by Angie Y. Crouch

Copyright © 2020

Welcome to Daufuskie

Daufuskie Island is one of South Carolina's best kept secret. The only way to get to the island is by boat or passenger ferry.

dock
boat
water

The ferry can carry many people. Most ferries have air conditioning in the summer months when it is warm, which is the busiest time of year.

seat
friends

The ferry ride lasts about forty-five minutes. People carry their luggage and food on the ferry if they plan to stay overnight. Some guests even bring their dogs on the ferry ride. Travelers that want to reach Daufuskie Island faster can ride water taxi boats, which can take up to ten minutes.

golf cart
family

Only people that live on the island can have cars. Visitors are required to rent golf carts or ride bikes. The golf carts use gasoline and are very fast. Don't worry! Only adults with a license are allowed to drive the golf carts!

Freeport
General Store
bicycle

All golf carts are rented from the Freeport General Store on Daufuskie Island. People can also buy food, clothing, gifts, and gas at the store. This is the only place on the island that sells supplies.

power nap
golf cart

The roads on Daufuskie Island are not like highways in the city. Most roads are made of dirt or have very narrow paved lanes. Look out when you're traveling! You will see special squirrels that live in the trees called Grey Fox Squirrels. They have lived on the island for a long time.

deer
horse
ranch

It can take about two hours to drive around the whole island on a golf cart. While riding or walking on the island you will see many wild animals. There is even a horse ranch on the island. Visitors can schedule horseback riding tours with guides.

turtle tracks
sand

The loggerhead turtle is one of the most popular animals on the island. Females lay their eggs mostly at night or early in the morning on the beach. You can see their tracks in the sand.

baby
turtle
eggs
2
LOGGERHEAD
TURTLE NESTING
AREA

After the loggerhead turtle lays her eggs, the nest is marked with a sign. The sign warns people that there is a turtle nest on the beach. It is against the law to touch the baby turtles!

hermit crab
shell
claws

Hermit crabs can also be found on Daufuskie Island. They come in all sizes. Be careful if you pick up one! It might pinch your finger!

shrimp

Shrimp can be found on the beach each morning after the tide goes down. There are many shrimp fishing boats out during the day. Watch out for the birds! They love to eat the shrimp for breakfast!

sand
claws
blue crab

Another animal that lives on Daufuskie Island is the blue crab. The blue crab likes to eat oysters and freshly dead fish, which may wash onto shore after the tide goes down.

water shoes

While exploring the beach, some people wear special water shoes to protect their feet. You never know where a hermit crab or a jellyfish might be hiding!

wave

The best part about the beach are the waves. The waves are small on the island, which is great for children. Watch closely and you might see some local dolphins swimming by!

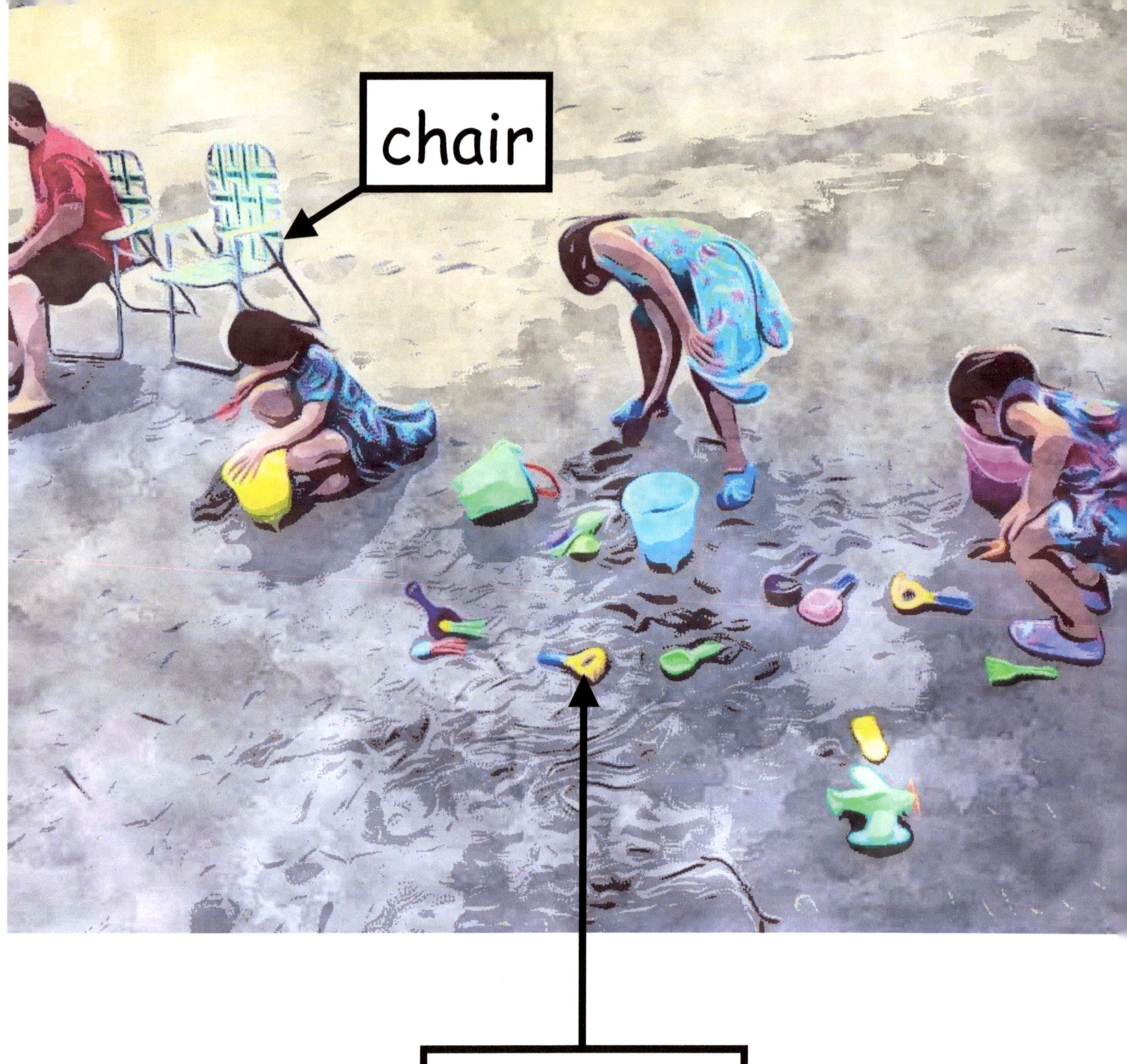

chair
sand toys

After playing in the waves some children like to play in the sand. Make sure you pack plenty of sand toys if you visit the beach!

shell
legs
horseshoe crab

While playing in the sand you might find some horseshoe crabs on the shore. Many of the horseshoe crabs look dead, but their shells are actually empty. As they grow they shed their shell and form a new one, leaving their old shell on the beach.

rock
alligator
swamp

After playing on the beach you can go for a ride and find the ponds where the alligators live. Be careful not to get too close! There are many baby alligators in the ponds and they can be seen swimming and eating.

Lucy Bell's
Cafe

After playing in the sand and looking for alligators, people can visit Lucy Bell's Cafe. It is one of the many great restaurants on the island. Lucy Bell's Cafe has been featured on TV for their great food. Even local celebrities like to eat there.

Bloody Point
Lighthouse

The restaurants aren't the only attractions. There are several lighthouses on Daufuskie Island. Bloody Point has a lighthouse that sells gifts and snacks. The lighthouse is very old and visitors can go on a tour!

Inside the lighthouse

Angel Oak
Tree

While visiting the Bloody Point Lighthouse, you can see the Angel Oak Tree on the property. The Angel Oak is very old and large. People can enjoy the vineyards on the nature walk to the tree.

Melrose swimming pool

After a long day of exploring the island, many people like to relax at the Melrose Beach Club & Pool! They have two pools, one for children and one for adults. While enjoying the pools, guests can eat at the Melrose restaurant and listen to live music.

Daufuskie Island

Most people enjoy a nice walk on the beach after eating, swimming, or visiting the attractions. Watching the sunset is the best way to end the day!

School Grounds
Coffee
frappuccino

After a long day of playing and a good nights rest, people may wake up and go to School Grounds Coffee. They sell coffee, drinks, and homemade desserts. School Grounds Coffee was once a real one-room schoolhouse.

ATTITUDE ADJUSTMENT
BOULEVARD

Just around the corner from School Grounds Coffee, visitors can find Attitude Adjustment Boulevard. It is a great photo prop for teenagers or grumpy adults!

My name is Budd
I am a
Scarlet Macaw
I was born in
2009
I can live to be
years old
I am pretty t
look at bu
DON'T TOU
I BITE!!
Budd

Don't forget to visit the Glass House. Guests can find handmade jewelry among other things there. Budd greets people at the entrance!

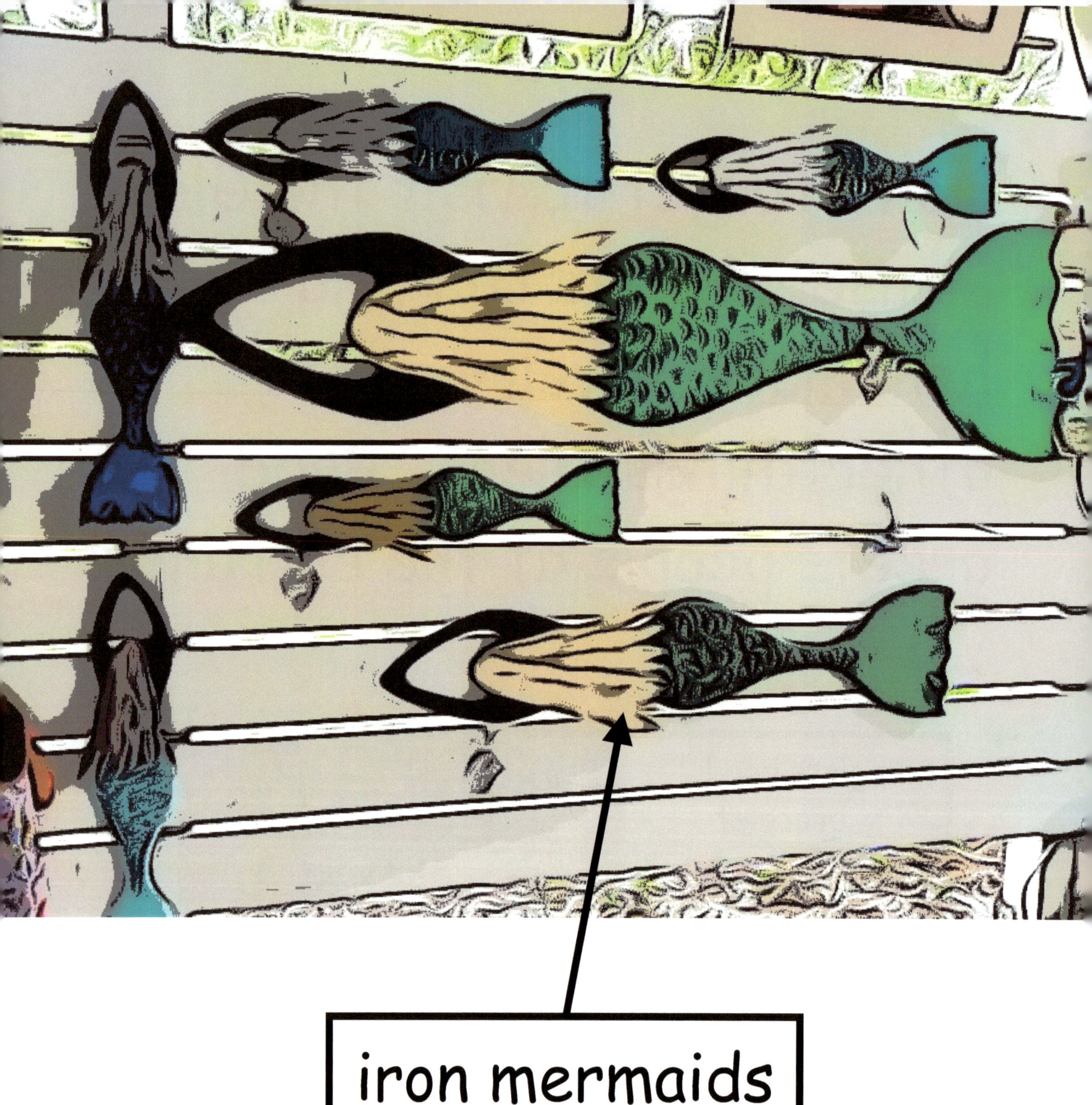

iron mermaids

Next, visitors can find the Iron Fish Gallery and Studio. The local sculptor makes all items by hand and his artwork is for sale. Shoppers can find iron mermaids, fish, turtles, and stingrays.

Daufuskie Island
History Museum

Lastly, you can visit the Daufuskie Island History Museum. It has many historical artifacts and books. Some of the artifacts include spears, pottery, and handmade furniture that date back thousands of years. They even have an alligator! Don't worry it isn't alive!

alligator

rental house
condos

Daufuskie Island is a hidden gem and truly a magical place! It allows people to leave their busy lives and become one with nature and history. Whether you come for the day, rent a house, or stay in a condo, it is a trip to remember!

Daufuskie Island,
South Carolina